The Life of
Ben Cohen
and the story of Ben & Jerry's ice cream

M.C. Hall

www.heinemann.co.uk/library

Visit our website to find out more information about **Heinemann Library** books.

To order:
- ☎ Phone 44 (0) 1865 888066
- 🖹 Send a fax to 44 (0) 1865 314091
- 💻 Visit the Heinemann Bookshop at www.heinemann.co.uk/library to browse our catalogue and order online.

First published in Great Britain by Heinemann Library, Halley Court, Jordan Hill, Oxford OX2 8EJ, part of Harcourt Education.
Heinemann is a registered trademark of Harcourt Education Ltd.

Editorial: Traci Todd and Harriet Milles
Design: Richard Parker and Maverick Design
Picture Research: Julie Laffin
Production: Camilla Smith

Originated by Repro Multi-Warna
Printed and bound in China by
    South China Printing Company

The paper used to print this book comes from sustainable resources.

ISBN 0 431 18099 7 (hardback)
09 08 07 06 05
10 9 8 7 6 5 4 3 2 1

ISBN 0 431 18158 6 (paperback)
10 09 08 07 06
10 9 8 7 6 5 4 3 2 1

British Library Cataloguing in Publication Data
M.C. Hall
Ben Cohen. – (The Life of)
338. 7'6374'092
A full catalogue record for this book is available from the British Library.

Acknowledgements
The Publishers would like to thank the following for permission to reproduce photographs:
p. **4** David Young-Wolff/Photo Edit; pp. **5, 23, 26** Getty Images; p. **6** Erich Hartmann/Magnum Photos; p. **7** Janet Lankford Moran/Heinemann Library; p. **8** Time Life Pictures/Getty Images; p. **9** Underwood & Underwood/Corbis; pp. **10, 11, 12** Corbis; p. **13** J. Graham/Robertstock.com; p. **14** Hulton Archive/Getty Images; p. **15, 18, 19** AP Wide World Photos; p. **16** James P. Blair/Corbis; p. **17** © Robert Grego. All rights reserved Vermont Photo Creations; p. **20** © Richard Levine; p. **21** Joe Sohm/The Image Works; p. **22** Andrew E. Cook; pp. **24, 27** Photri Microstock; p. **25** Robert Holmes/Corbis

Cover photograph by Getty Images
Cover and interior icons Janet Lankford Moran/Heinemann Library

Every effort has been made to contact copyright holders of any material reproduced in this book. Any omissions will be rectified in subsequent printings if notice is given to the Publishers.

Contents

Words shown in the text in bold, **like this**, are explained in the Glossary.

We all like ice cream!

People all over the world love ice cream. This cold treat comes in lots of different flavours. People eat ice cream in cones, bars, and as a sweet.

Ice cream is one of the world's favourite foods!

When he was a young boy, Ben Cohen loved ice cream. When he grew up, he started an ice cream **company** with his best friend, Jerry Greenfield. They made and sold **unusual** flavours of ice cream.

This is Ben on the right, with his best friend Jerry.

The early years

Ben Cohen was born in Brooklyn, New York, USA, in 1951. His father was an **accountant**. His mother looked after Ben and his sister. When Ben was young, the family moved to Merrick, New York.

This is what Brooklyn looked like in the 1950s.

Ben and his father both loved ice cream.
Ben's father could eat a whole tub-full
after dinner!

Ben liked to
add things, like
pieces of
biscuit and
chocolate, to
his ice cream.

Ben meets Jerry

When Ben was 12 years old, he became best friends with Jerry Greenfield. During the summers, they earned money by sorting the post at the office of Ben's father.

Ben and Jerry liked going to the nearby beach with their friends.

In his last year at school, Ben got a job driving an ice cream van, selling ice cream. In 1969, he started college at Colgate University in Hamilton, New York.

Ben sold his ice cream from a van like this one.

College years

Ben did not like college, so he left and travelled to California. He worked there as an ice cream seller. After a few months, he went back to New York.

Ben got a job driving taxis just like these all over New York.

Ben enjoyed making clay pots.

Ben went to **pottery** and jewellery classes at Skidmore College in Saratoga Springs, New York. In 1972, he moved to New York City to work as a potter.

A teaching job

In 1974, Ben started to teach at a school for troubled teenagers. He taught them **pottery**, photography, film making, and other **crafts**.

The school was close to the Adirondack mountains in New York State.

On the right is an ice cream maker. Ben used one like this to make ice cream for the school children.

Ben also worked as the school cook. Sometimes he made ice cream for the school children. In 1976, the school closed. Ben was out of a job again.

13

Looking for ideas

Ben and his old friend, Jerry Greenfield, decided to start a **company** together. Ben and Jerry both liked eating! They wanted to have a food company.

Ben and Jerry knew that other people liked eating too!

Here are Jerry and Ben
scooping ice cream.

At first, Ben and Jerry thought that they
would open a restaurant. Then they
decided that they wanted to make and
sell ice cream instead.

Getting started

Ben and Jerry looked for a place to start their **company**. They chose Burlington, Vermont. There were no **ice cream parlours** in Burlington. Theirs would be the first.

There is a big university in Burlington. Ben and Jerry knew that students liked ice cream!

Ben and Jerry borrowed money to buy an old petrol station. They spent months fixing it up. They also took classes to learn more about making ice cream.

The old petrol station is not there any more. Today there is only this plaque in the pavement to show where it was.

The first ice cream parlour

Ben & Jerry's Homemade **Ice Cream Parlour** opened on 5 May 1978. It served **unusual** ice cream flavours, such as *Coconut and Honey Almond Mist*. People tried the ice cream, and loved it.

This is the first Ben & Jerry's ice cream parlour in Burlington.

At first Ben and Jerry did most of the jobs themselves. When the **company** grew, they moved into a bigger space.

Soon Ben and Jerry started selling their ice cream to grocery shops.

Ben & Jerry's grows

Other people wanted to start their own Ben & Jerry's **ice cream parlours**. They paid Ben and Jerry money so that they could use the Ben & Jerry's name.

This is the first shop that was allowed to use the Ben & Jerry's name. It opened in Shelbourne, Vermont in 1981.

This is the Ben & Jerry's factory in Waterbury, Vermont.

In 1986, Ben and Jerry opened a **factory** near Waterbury, Vermont. They sold so much ice cream that they soon opened another factory in Springfield, Vermont.

Helping others

Ben and Jerry decided that their **company** would give away some of the money it made every year. The money would go to help people and groups in the **community**.

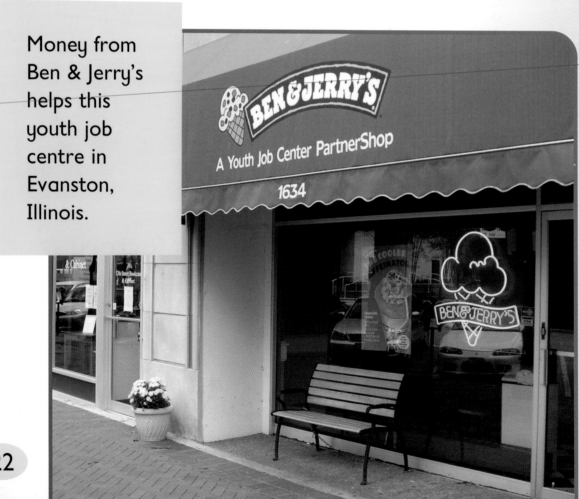

Money from Ben & Jerry's helps this youth job centre in Evanston, Illinois.

In 2002, Ben made a new ice cream flavour called *One Sweet Whirled*. Here he is eating some with US Senator Jim Jefford (right).

Ben also believes that companies should work to save the **environment**. He used rain forest nuts in his ice cream, so that people would not cut down the nut trees.

The later years

Ben and Jerry wanted their workers to be happy and have fun. They won awards for the way that they ran their **company**, and for helping the **environment**.

Every year, Ben and Jerry liked to meet the people who supported their company.

In 2000, Ben and Jerry sold their **business** to a large food company. Ben does not work for Ben & Jerry's Ice Cream now. He still does **community** work to help people.

Ben and Jerry's famous Cowmobile travels around to many community **projects**.

Ben today

Today, Ben works hard for a group that he started called True Majority. True Majority tries to get **laws** passed by the US **government** that will help children, the **environment**, and the world.

Ben makes speeches to get people to **vote** on paper – not on computers. He wants to make sure that every person's vote is counted.

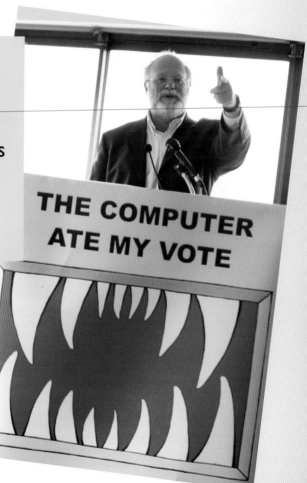

THE COMPUTER ATE MY VOTE

Ben & Jerry's ice cream is famous all over the world. You can learn more about the **company** by visiting the **factory** near Waterbury, Vermont.

This is the Ben & Jerry's factory in Waterbury, Vermont. Here people can see how the ice cream is made.

Fact file

- Ben says that he and Jerry were the 'slowest, fattest kids' in their class at school!

- Ben and Jerry took classes by post to learn how to make ice cream. The classes cost them five US dollars.

- In 1999, Ben & Jerry's celebrated 21 years of ice-cream making by giving away ice cream across the USA. The **company** gave away more than half a million ice-cream cones!

- Ben Cohen was married for a while. He and his former wife, Cindy, have one daughter, named Aretha.

- One of Ben's hobbies is riding motorbikes. He likes to ride around the countryside in Vermont.

Timeline

1951	Ben Cohen is born in Brooklyn, New York
1963	Ben meets Jerry Greenfield
1972	Ben moves to New York City
1978	Ben and Jerry open their first **Ice Cream Parlour** in Burlington, Vermont
1980	Ben and Jerry start selling ice cream to grocery shops
1985	Ben and Jerry build an ice cream **factory** near Waterbury, Vermont. Ben and Jerry start the Ben & Jerry's Foundation to give away money for **community projects**.
1994	Ben & Jerry's begins selling ice cream in the UK
1995	Ben and Jerry open a new factory in St. Albans, Vermont
2000	Ben and Jerry sell the ice cream company

Glossary

accountant person who keeps track of money for a business

business activity that earns money

company group of people who make money by selling things

community town or city where people live or work

craft making things by hand, such as pots or jewellery

environment the world around you. Water, plants, and air are all part of the environment.

factory building in which things are made

government group that leads a country and makes laws

ice cream parlour place where people can buy and eat ice cream

law the rules of a country

pottery making things, like dishes and pots, from clay

project plan of work to help other people

unusual strange

vote give support to something or someone

Find out more

Books

Ben and Jerry's Homemade Ice Cream and Dessert Book, Ben Cohen (Workman Publishing, 1991)

The Ultimate Ice Cream Book, Bruce Weinstein (William Morrow, 1999)

The Ice Cream Machine Book, Rosemary Moon (Apple Press, 2001)

Websites

www.benjerry.co.uk

Ben & Jerry's UK website contains lots of fun activities and information about ice cream.

Places to visit

Ben & Jerry's Ice Cream Factory, Waterbury, Vermont, USA.

Always remember that eating too much ice cream is bad for your health.

Index